Essay Stanzas

Thomas Meyer

The Song Cave

Published by The Song Cave
www.the-song-cave.com
© 2014 Thomas Meyer
Author photo: Reuben Cox
Design and layout by Mary Austin Speaker

ISBN 0-9884643-5-7
Library of Congress Control Number: 2014948005
FIRST EDITION

Table of Contents

Essay Stanzas

What is dreamt, it is proposed, has no more claim to sense and meaning than, for instance, the sounds which would be produced if "the ten fingers of someone who knows nothing about music were wandering over the keys of a piano."

Sigmund Freud, *On Dreams*

CAUGHT BETWEEN

This won't amount to much.
A handful of flowers
put on the table.
A souvenir unheard, unseen.

Morning, noon, and night.
The sky's gems.

Dawn upon the hills? No!
Bright Cinderella
rises from Sleeping Beauty's thigh.
A thousand blind eyes.

She hides her eyes
behind a bright veil.
And under her breath:
"I am afraid of men."

Sometimes the gods
write on the wide blue sky
with lightning. Strange alphabets

I can't read or make sense of
yet I still want to know
what they say. I still want to read
what they write.

The sky reaches out
to hold me.
East, west, north, south:
wide open.
But I am wrapped up
in myself.

What exactly is this sky?
Hot? Cold? Overcast?
Do we really see it?
Is it ever really there?
Or is it an actress
playing the part god wrote for her
but adding extra bits of her own?

"Has Jack the Giant Killer gulped down the ocean again?
Have the valleys opened up and leveled the mountains?"
wonders the sky, swallowing a big black ball of opium.
His eyes roll back in happy blindness
as he lowers himself down.

What did we see
in the dark? Up there.
Not a cloud. No. A tiny spark.
A black fleck on
the liquid cheek
of his Queen.

When I look up at that dark blue sky
made all the more beautiful
by a great big black cloud,
it's my good luck to see the bruise
Abraham's foot left on Isaac's chest.

This isn't sunrise, is it?
This is the wealth the gods possess.
This can't be the sun! No,
this is a bowl of honey.
These aren't clouds, red, yellow, purple. No,
these are gods and devils fighting it out.
Look, some pair of invisible hands
is making from the sky the story of how
everything came to be: "Churning Up the Milky Sea."

That great light chased away by dark
from dirt to tree tops

down alpine slopes
off to the back of beyond.
Then suddenly it returns to
all that shines in the night sky
to wait for time to let it go.

These stars' black seeds
fall on night's dark ground.
Look, they flower:
early morning light.

All earth wrapped
in thick dark. Light
shoved aside
looks the other way.
While his spies, the stars,
wait and watch.

I know what I see
in this world is a trick of light,
nevertheless I want to watch
this beautiful illusion's
eyes open and lips part.

Each of the four directions seek my attention.
There in the east is dawn taking a bath.
Handsome west is red-faced and drunk.
I listen to the north recite formal verse.
Aggressive and various, the south
stands where Buddha's foot
crushed ignorance.
And I'm pulled this way and that
though earth has pinned me to my spot,
rootless as a tree.

When night comes, day fascinates.
The dark makes light bright.
Likewise 'shade' and 'sunshine'
name the same thing.

Night discloses.
Day is straight forward.
Night hesitates
and shows us each bit by bit
like a song.
The sun, the moon, the others:
light coming down, moving across, going out
withstanding time's approach.
Yes, but wind, you alone fill

this huge space
however you choose, whenever
you please. No wonder they call you the sky's.
You bring down trees and break branches.
But other times you're hardly there,
nothing more than a ripple of air,
a dust cloud.
Yes, you have your bad side,
but that isn't what draws us to you.
Everything stale is fresh again
because of you. Because of you
things are clearer and brighter.

Clouds row across the lake of sky
above this mountain
whose base is cemented to the ground
and like a poet, head lost in the cloud.
Feet planted firmly on the ground,
he is pulled in opposite directions
and rails against his immobility
with a stream of noisy complaints
which are also the sad sound of running water.

At that time of year when it rains
this mountain puts on a royal blue and green coat.
In the summer he dresses in grasses

worn-out, threadbare, colorless.
Either season his natural stature, his flawless dignity
remain in tact. It makes sense to call him "resolute."

The ocean stirs up huge clouds
which Jesus lifts into the sky.
The mountains remember god's anger,
when he clipped their wings
so they block the clouds.
But being stuck in one
place
their fury made worse by their powerlessness
remains fruitless. Nevertheless they persevere.

"Have we suddenly got our wings back?
Those huge wings we lost to Jesus so long ago?
And can we really fly again across the horizon,
changing into whatever we want, whenever we want?"
These sad, eager mountains look up at the billowing clouds
and imagine wings budding in the crags of their backs.

This peak
could be Paul Bunyan's
hand turned to stone
fixed by the lion's gaze.

Or it could be
a hand held up
into the wide sky
by the mountain himself
to test the force of the wind.

Does the doe
leaping on the ground
even imagine
in her wildest dreams
what the mountain
with his head in the silent sky
sees — even though
he's caught in one spot?

Say, my friend,
cloud,
you embezzle the sea's capital
steadily
but please sidestep this peak.
The earth holds out her hand
hoping for whatever she can
from the likes of you.

Ah, cloud, now no bigger than a hand,
then suddenly a Goliath.
Are you acting out David's life?
Here a dwarf, there a cosmos.
Nevertheless, you do all this
with skill lost on the blind.

Cloud, desert sands ask you
for just a glance. But you waste
your gifts on the mountains
the minute you give them.
Generous of you? Maybe, but
anything given without a thought
as to who does or does not deserve it
instantly loses its immediate worth.

This earth so huge
yet so wobbly.
So its creator
implanted mountains
for support.

Lightning rips through the cloud
who weeps helplessly
and wants to die on the spot.

The nagging housewife strikes terror.
She holds the upper hand.
Don't believe it when the cloud
claims to be able to handle lightning.
All that's heaped up on you
and you carry through the sky,
backbreaking, slowly
like an emblem of
us on earth and
our struggle. Though there's
a major difference for you.
Everywhere you turn
someone in these mountains
is there to share your heartache.
For us on earth even a single
sympathetic soul is rare.
Yet trouble keeps coming,
getting steadily worse, day after day.

About to give birth, a belly full of water,
this fat, indifferent, hard-hearted cloud
wanders above, robbing peacocks and young butterflies
of their hope. Though the thirsty pray,
their prayers go unanswered.
A past life stamps this cloud
with his ocean parents' tight fists.

The glib extol the natural wealth of this cloud,
but I know how he secretly cheats the ocean
while he openly, with much fanfare,
doles out his ill-gotten gains. No surprise
he tries to shut me up and threatens me
with bolts of lightning.

Now, cloud, this monsoon season
nothing much to you today,
no moisture, nothing to give.
No more than a toy for the wind.
And your good friend lightning has left you.
Who wants to be a friend to the poor?
But then you never gave much thought
to anything other than showing off.
So when you've got it, spread it all over.
When it's gone, you'll have time to think.

He watches his friends, clouds, blown apart
by Jehovah's lightning bolt, and this compassionate mountain
weeps gushing streams. But this isn't a mountain.
This is King Lear himself whose deep and ancient sorrow
suddenly bursts into poetry.
A Cupid pierced by the hunter's arrow.
Solemn omen.

This lamp all on his own
burned to wipe out some small part
of black night, to make it happy
with his oily tongue, his wick.
But now without much ado
the rising sun puts him out.

The little flame of this lamp
burns steady and bright
tonight in this cabin,
and seems, somehow, more powerful
than the sudden lightning flash
breaking the darkness a second
but leaving it even blacker
as it vanishes.

The lamp's light
isn't worried about the darkness
surrounding it.
But closes its startled eyes
to the creatures of the night

Look, these bright street lamps,
at the same time, set alight
opposite directions without

favoring one way or the other.
Is this complete indifference a virtue?
Or is it the natural consequence
of that dark they take away?

Near a lamp, shadows move away,
and shrink when the light is above,
although they are pestered like this,
shadows like faithful employees
never abandon us, whom they work for.

My shadow, I used to think,
backed me up from behind.
Now I realize
I am my shadow's human shield.

The noisy stream trickling down
the mountain alone,
afraid calls out: "The sea, my good friend,
too far away for comfort —
while here the brutal woods
threaten me, alone and helpless."

Why does this loaded down stream
chatter and crow about the gifts
he bears for the mountain
to the ocean, from a lord
to his king?

Cloud, can you name
a single creek
who in your wandering
hasn't become talkative
because of your rain?

People forced to run after themselves
tripping over their own feet at every step,
just so, coming and going seem the same.
They are both called celebrities by the wise.

Running after the horizon
completely exhausts me —
and for nothing…
But why can't you see
the outlook it affords?

Ah, horizon, the logical and practical say,
planted on wide mountain plateaus,
caressing the surf, holding the earth close,
you are nothing more than an illusion.
Not there. Forever withdrawn.
That being so, continuing to search for your edge,
sometimes it seems like a good idea
to go on and on and on.

This ocean reflecting the sky's movement
spreads out in front of me
and displays faces looking down from above.
So it makes sense, his name, "Box of Gems"
and not just figuratively.
The ocean can rise up in anger
and dash about wealthy yachts
and at other times bring a tiny raft
to safe haven on his quiet waves
with a remarkable tenderness.
Either way, there's something inside him,
the same thing a good actor has,
that leaves him completely uninvolved
with what's going on outside him.

Look, ocean, at how fishermen
skip all over your waves,

and cast nets whenever they want
into your depth, then haul up thousands of fish
who are still in your care.
They stand on your shores, these men,
among heaps of fish bones, and complain
about you, rail against you.
Even so, you are the protector of whatever
lives in your waters. Or so
we're told.

"Missouri's daughter, you are worth more to me
than life. Columbia, you are life itself!"
he tells his wives, these rivers
spread out all across the earth.
Putting on the look of love. Maybe
too theatrical, a little too knowing
nevertheless you have to ask yourself,
is this ocean's genius?
Actor
or grifter?

The thirsty walk away
looking for something to drink
somewhere else.
While treasure seekers
are sent packing by this slinky ocean's

underwater glitter.
Only the sun knows how to
mine this resource,
gentle at times with tender shafts of light,
overwhelming at other times with blasts of fire,
turning this brine into nourishment.

The entire ocean held in the small of his hand,
Jonah drank it down with one big gulp.
So, millions of rivers running endlessly into
that empty space he left there
even after millennium upon millennium
can't fill it.

A heaving tidal horizon fills my eyes
when suddenly it occurs to me
a tear has appeared upon the seam
of sky and sea, flapping open in the wind
letting me look at what lies outside all this.
Though suddenly a huge wave rises up
in anger before me and blinds me forever.

The ocean every day gives away
much of all he has. Yet, for whatever reason,
perhaps his carelessness, he's called a penny-pincher.

While King Cole himself amasses more and more to hoard
and surprisingly has this reputation for being such a great benefactor.

A fine spray is how the ocean offers the clouds
his water. They, in turn, have the reputation
of being "water bearers."
While he is criticized for a seeming lack of generosity.
Though he takes it all in his stride,
his largesse goes unfelt, and remains invisible.
Who else is there like this? This philanthropist of the brine?

All you have, ocean, has been appropriated
by the gods and devils,
who have also run off with the wine
meant to ease your sorrow for their plundering.
Even the lethal poison
which you planned to swallow
and thus be released from this loss, that
has been stolen.
Surely, the irony in all this remains
that despite whatever your ruin
you are still called "rich with treasure!"

Poems tell us about the modesty of trees
bent down under the weight of their fruit

but if the truth be known, they groan
overloaded with the responsibility
of taking care of and protecting
their large families, all those branches, and leaves and ...

Ah, heavy with fruit, this tree, in a public place,
that passers-by scrape and bump into
without giving it a thought,
wishes to be a thorn of some kind.

Sun or moon, it doesn't matter,
even the darkness, or whatever it is,
just as long as it is
powerful and new,
the trees give into it instantly,
each and every one,
their heads held down
by its sudden foot.

That helpless tree there
the light rains upon
whose roots grab the earth
reminds me of Sebastian himself
attacked by arrows,
hands tied behind his back.

"The ground under me grabs my feet —
well, actually, swallows them.
The wind messes up my hair —
well, actually, it yanks it right out.
But what hurts me the most — me, a tree!
— is that in all four directions the air
points, and waves, and laughs at me."

This huge, towering tree stands in the desert
alone, and hears
every now and then a rustling,
a little dry patch of grass.
Looking all around, as far as his eye sees
there's nothing that reminds him of himself.
So is his sorrow for being so tall.
Alone, who does he have to talk to
but the gray, unwelcoming sky.

Fig tree, the least stirrings of the air
you respond to with slight quivering,
and motion to the clouds,
reaching up, peering into the distance.
How… no, "who" has taught you
this exquisite sensitivity?

Flame azalea, your leaves' new green
are like parakeet wings,
your bright flowers like beaks.
So much so, that flocks of parakeets
watch you in fear from the forest,
thinking you must be Papageno's trap.

Pine, you clean and purify
and freshen and heal
but your bitterness
distracts.

Men sit safe and sound in the garden,
protected by a cactus hedge
and without a second thought
ask the cactus, "Where are your flowers?
Your fruit? Your leaves? Why are you so bare,
so distant, and thorny? Who wants to get near you?
What good are you to us?"

"The sandalwood's perfume pleases
even the axe's gleaming blade
ready to chop him to pieces.
Solomon was never more fragrant."
Too bad, the sandalwood

completely intoxicated by such flattery
can't see the sly smile
on the face of the man
with an axe.

Sandalwood,
when you fragrantly bless the axe's blade
it seems to me
you are only sharpening it.
The turtle still thinks
"Once, long ago, taking the shape of a turtle,
Merlin picked up the earth from the flood
and left it to us,
making us his lawful heirs."
And that turtle hardly able to drag himself
across the ground goes on and on
about this promise made to his kind,
that they, and they alone, would bear
the weight of this earth on their backs.

The rooster wonders
"Who makes the sun
get up and do his job?"
While in the kitchen
the book lies open
to *coq au vin*.

The Buddha aside,
thankless us
who ignore
dawn's messenger
can't see
how this world
is soon to be thrust
into timeless dark.

This deer
leaps through
the same electric, fragrant air
that eventually will be
his nervous ruin.

Camel, men call you "ugliness itself,"
hate you and make fun of you.
Even at an oasis you eat thorns
but hold enough water to last for days.
Careful, my friend, these caravans
take you with them, charm and sweet-talk you,
call you "desert schooner."
I only hope
that when they are scorched and thirsty
they don't remember
all that water in your hump.

A deer who'd been
tricked once too often
by mirage
came upon an actual pool
but turned and walked away
not touching a drop,
gasping for water
determined not be made a fool of again.

The camel walking through the sands
has for a long time in himself
the water no one saw him drink.
The coconut lying on the sands
beside the sea contains
water he drank long ago.

Grand elephant,
solemn and ceremonious
the loud golden bell
around your throat
rings out.
What's not apparent to you
is the drowned out
laughter of
the man riding on your head.

The famished lion in his cage
snatches at rotten meat, maybe,
or bones picked clean
from some starved dog
who died long ago
and has stunk ever since
— even that!
But he tosses it away almost immediately,
angry because he hears
inside himself an elephant
in the wild
laughing at him.

Although the lion's been gone
from this mountain side
for quite awhile,
the elephant herd
moves toward his den
with utmost fear and tembling.

"I'll tear apart
even the biggest of elephants
when I get him,"
brags the lion king
who once sharpened his claws
on rocks in the woods —

but today just scratches himself
with those claws, chained up
in a narrow cage.

For years this unusual horse
out in the hills had heard of
the king's splendid stable
and wanted to go see these
famous brothers of his.
And he did. And he saw
animals very different from himself
and was very impressed with
what he saw when
the man at the door started
to beat him with a big stick
yelling, "What's this donkey
from the hills
doing in here?"

Doesn't make sense:
here is the donkey,
patience itself,
whose every move
is made with
absolute indifference—
an enlightened being.

He pays no attention
to aches and pains
but still he's known as
stubborn.

Cuckoos dart and land
on branches in well tended gardens.
A little embarrassed,
they watch their own,
happy and plump,
taken care of by crows.
And the cuckoos sing "ckoo-ckoo." Happy-go-
lucky, untroubled by anything, nothing
else mattering much.
God let these shameless birds
live a good and long life, a hundred years
of give and take
in someone else's
cherry trees.

A man had heard how swans
can drink just the milk
and leave the water
when the two are mixed.
So he brought home a swan
to see if this was so

and when it did just that,
the neighborhood milkman
said, "Look! Nothing but water is left.
At least when I make my rounds
there's a bit of milk in it!"

An overcast sky,
an earth in shadow,
and nothing visible
in any direction.
Muddy woods
filled with frogs croaking.
Yet on this dark and rainy day
you can see peacocks
doing a mating dance
trying to be like
that flash of lightning
that shears the black cloud.

"Oh, I could never eat like this
out there in the woods?
Isn't this to be free, to wait
in this beautiful cage
on a solid gold bar
for all the delicacies
brought to me?"

But then a light breeze
slightly ruffles
the parrot's feathers
and he cocks his head
towards those woods
where it comes from.

Catbird on the highest branch,
staring straight at the cloud
you lift your head,
straight-necked,
for that single water drop.
If only you knew
how corrupt this world is.
There in the pond
watch the clever cranes,
secret and cunning.
They go where they like
in the muddy water,
their heads bent,
their eyes see nothing else.

Devious stork, eyes shut tight,
hunts fish whose eyes are wide open,
always making fun of the ever attentive,

all seeing world looking up
from under his pale white belly.

The fish, his eyes never shut
looking everywhere, and despite this,
he's hypnotized by
the fatal hook —
welcome lure
of constant watchfulness.

The bee ignores all these apple blossoms,
could care less for the blackberries in bloom,
he's only interested in their sweetness,
nonetheless he's famous for being
such a lover of their bouquets.

The frog who all his life has heard
the eagle praised for his command of the skies
jumps up at the edge of his small pond
which reflects a little bit of blue heaven
and he croaks, he honks, he pokes fun.

This clever side-winding snake
tries to break the earth's heart

by making deep holes in it.
This redwood tree
reaches up to calculate
how far the sky is —
his own height is his measure.

With the whole world on his back,
Atlas, completely worn out, groans
and his groans turn into snakes, hissing,
wicked and stinking.

Kings, some say, prop up the earth —
well, they also say mountains do too,
but, in fact, the truth is the earth
supports them both.
So too, it is Jack's giant, by himself,
who takes almost no notice
and carries the whole world on his back.

Looking the other way and dodging
Abaham's thousand restless eyes,
these snakes, with their poisonous hisses,
turn the patriarch's bright white skinned son
black as night in the flick of an eye.
No wonder their earthly opposite numbers

can make the untouched, or that which is
as white as milk as black as mud.

Snake, we know all about your love of music
and sweet smells. But, I'm afraid, all this
loses its meaning to the poison you carry.

People talk about the wickedness of snakes,
but isn't it the huge snake in the night sky
who allows everything in creation
the moment it draws breath.

An urban sprawl of tiny ants
going about their business,
all contained inside this heap
outdoing these hills and mountains
which contain nothing
but a load of dead stones.

Assuming this must be Christ himself
swallowing the darkness
while putting forth light,
the devout moth
flies into the lamp's bright flame,

and, too bad, is now no more than
a speck of ash. Pray for his soul,
he didn't know
that both the good and the bad,
the devil and the god, wise men tell us,
must be worshiped
at a distance.

When the worms wriggling in black caves —
they've never seen the sun's splendor,
nor soft moonlight — spotted a firefly
they exploded in amazement.
"Look! Here by the grace of god,
Christ himself returns to earth
in fresh raiment, yielding a disc of light
to bless us all!"

Noticing that
the money man used potatoes to weigh gold
the silly wife urged her husband to plant a crop
then noticing that
they tasted better than gold
she suddenly found herself
completely satisfied.

Touchstone, your mark tells
true gold or genuine silver,
your skill unquestioned.
Even so, you can't get rid of the fact
that you yourself are only stone.

Philosopher's stone, who else
in this world can make black iron white gold?
But there's a problem here.
When other metals talk to each other
about fair and unfair,
your name heads the list — they all agree...
the list of those completely biased.

If you can hear or understand
a word I say,
stone, refuse the divinity
imposed upon you by the simple and scheming.
Don't let the flower garlands chain you,
or the dark temple be your prison cell —
yes, they will accuse you
of stealing what little the poor have.

Your tides, coming up then running away,
their white foam and blue green ripples

make the statue of the Virgin smile.
She holds a ship in her arms.

Johnny Appleseed scared long ago
by Paul Bunyan's plough
goes all weak at the knees
when he sees the farmwives'
black eyebrows raised.
They look like ploughs
and they look like swords.

Writers, O Mighty Mississippi, complain
that you rise and fall, sometimes clear
but more often muddy
which I think has its own splendor.
It somehow blesses life itself
rather than proposing lucid
but shallow simplicities.

My god, the poor sea!
That mill churning out salt
beneath those depths,
washing his wounds
which burn and burn.

Millennia of agony
we can read into those tides.

The trees nod. The wind
tells them secrets.
They agree. My heart
can't help overhearing
what they say, and try as I might, I
can't stop listening.

KEPT APART

"Who else but some great big pronoun
can stand my furious come-on?"
Just so she comes to earth
making these crazy allegations.
When suddenly all of her
flood and flow gets swallowed up
by nothing more than a man.

All that he gave up
broke open heaven's gates
blinding me the way
a lightning flash can.

I won't ask
where in god's name
your dead relatives are.
One for each glass of water.
Though I do know
the rivers you brought
endlessly care for
orchards forever.

Surprised but satisfied with what he's done.
Asleep. All alone.
Nonetheless the gods laugh
because the road to heaven is blocked.
Who cares? Halfway there.
Damn them. Here is earth.
Dear earth.

Looking up at the stars.
At how they veer
unattached to anything visible
upon an unsupported black sky.
Nothing upholds
any worrying about this.

Don't let it bother you,
your plunge from bright skies
or split from meager earth.
Be thankful instead
for this almost innocent state
astride above and below
solidly hung upon the air.
Something no man, no woman, no god
knows how to do.
Nor has earned the right to.

Once upon a time
there was a king
who made a promise in his sleep
and kept it
until the day he died.
But look at us,
we can hardly remember what we said
in a dream
much less
wide awake
in daylight.

Good sir,
I am honored by your visit.
But I'm having a hard time
understanding what you say.
Maybe if you
slowed down,
or started at the beginning?
Excuse me, I forget.
You could be coming
from one long dream
to another
where you'll be king.
"Go to hell." He said. Turned.
And disappeared
in the ground

in a burst of flame
in a whiff of brimstone.

She has gone back to heaven
having conquered me entirely.
Here I am on earth trying to recover.
Every broken vow. Each promise I made.
Here. Then gone. Like a dream.
I rolled myself into a ball ashamed
and hid like an owl at noon.
Though none the wiser.
I've lost everything good.
She has completely done me in.
Totally humiliated me.

He meant to make a new world
beyond even god's imagining.
However, she
on the other hand
ignites his passion
and he confuses
above and below
falling like new mown hay
in a heap on the ground
still twitching in the wind.

I've never done
anything
as hard as this.
I doubt god has.
Even so
my mind is reeling.
Struck down
at her feet.
Thinking this
he failed to notice
his most treasured dream
had disappeared
along with her.

Sons killed before your own eyes.
Cattle run off into the woods.
None of this catches you off balance.
Watching you has been a revelation.
A birth. Twice-born am I.
I throw off my old title:
World-hater.
And take a new one:
World-lover.

He asked the king
to give up both his sons

in order to secure
sound protection.
"But how can I risk
my left and my right arms?"
So he turned and walked away
taking a last look
at the bow the king
cradled in the crook of his right arm.

He had dreamed
again and again
of this place in the woods.
And when he actually got there
he asked,
What's the next step?
"Let your foot fall
upon my heart
forever."

When the arrow left his bow
the empty sky boomed
and flat earth rumbled
with the news
that he was dead.
It had come to this.

He turned and faced the mountain
and wept. Happy.
Unhappy.

In the same exact moment
the former body dies
and the new is born.
What to do? Cry or laugh?
A sword's edge.
Sing. Sing with a lump in your throat.
Loud. The winner declared.
The hot tears of grief.
The cold tears of joy.

Two great lights
completely independent
of anything that came
before them when they
rose and set the earth
shook shocked to see
twin suns
rise and set
at the same time
upon the mountains.

"Why? After all these years
why did you take the millstone
from around my neck?
My waking death
and make me go back through
my humiliating life."
Unable to look him in the eye
she railed against him
in her unhappiness and disappointment.

All the time his sons
ran back and forth around him
the memory of that awful curse
rose like an awakened cobra.
Confused, shaken
hearing the boys' footsteps
asks himself,
"No, these can't be
death's walking
this direction."

That hand
that steered the car so well,
up and down,
hills and valleys,
that hand

fixed the car when it broke down,
turning into its axle,
that same hand
thrown away
mashed and twisted
in some dark corner
unheard of, forgotten.

"Car? You say a car,
a jet-black car has come?
Who sent it?
Is it here to take me
where I belong? I'll go."
And in he got
thinking he was on his way
to see his son
when in fact this car
had been sent
by Death to fetch him.

"Father, wait. Wait for me!"
The weeping and sobbing
continue to echo
through the house
for a long time after.
The sorrow suggests

a deeply embedded curse.
During all this
the car pulls off
and after a short while
the headlamps come on
to light the king's dark drive to heaven.

He goes toward the woods
with god and his brother
then upon them good wishes
and lavish blessings
fall from trembling hands
and tears making the makeup run
and the looking back.
They walk
as humans and guardians
disguised by the shadows
they cast.

Earth quakes
because of her daughter's
public shame
and accuses me.
The chair trembles
frightened of what I've done.
Walking toward it

fresh tears blinded him
and the short distance
from here to there
appeared rocky
as though the way
were to blame.

Eyes closed. He can see her
right before him
and in the woods
at the same moment.
The lilt of her voice
runs under
her heart breaking weeping.
Eyes shut. Ears, as well.
Old memories. Happy. Sad.
He blames himself.
And takes leaden steps
but doesn't budge.

"Why do you call me
after all these years
again?
And why do these
trees in a dream
say my name?"

She stands
dumbfounded
but still doesn't know.
The woods promise her
a place to go.
The last. The very last place
left for her to go.

"The bridge that spans this ocean
is my enemy's hand
reaching out
to touch my wife's thigh.
Or is she weeping
because of her husband's death?
Even though I am still alive."
And then he remembered
how passionately his enemy
loved his wife.

When he heard
how earth had
swallowed up his daughter
it drove him mad
and he took a plough
to till her back into being.
Maybe, he thought,

she'll come back
from wherever she went
to bring me back
my failing sight.

For his pleasure
the musician
hoisted a mountain up
to be his guitar or lute
whose strings were the sinews
from his own neck.
And just as this instrument was about to sound
god loaned him his emptied mind
to be its sounding board.

There was the serious demand
and grave need to gain a place
that made him choose sleep.
A night person.
The dark
whose thousand eyes
never close, they see, they watch.
These made him nervous.
Ceaseless insomnia.
He shuddered and chose sleep.
Good sleep.

The wind will tell you
what I'm doing on earth.
Clouds will broadcast news of me
in heaven.
He fell from above
and became a snake below
filled with desire
for someone else's wife
and an appetite for frogs.

In the woods he saw his children.
Snakes every last one of them.
I am both heaven and earth's lord!
Which of these do you want?

Look, his youth taken into old age.
Earth asks for a new leader.
But they reminded him of his vows.
So back to the wood he went
glancing over his shoulder
at the substantial house
he left.

"The woods?" He asked. "You want them?"
Yes. So he offered them up in flames.

Both were glad. One to have.
One to give.
While everything went up in smoke.
Screams and cries of animals.

They laughed
at him all done up
in sea shells.
But stopped laughing
when his arrows
flew all about them
shattering their armor.
Then heard him blow
the conch.

Overhead as far as the eye sees.
Blue. A river. Holy water.
Mountain tops blocking the gods.
Now this once was. But now evaporates.
Handful of smoke.
But she saw it all. A tender dream
whose unfolding she watches.

"Just look at this earth!
I am overjoyed

until the last of my days.
And above, the sky!
Let it fill my mind forever."
The girl in the shade of her desire
watched them struck by lightning.
Suddenly, out of the blue.
Now nothing more than charred stumps.

They say the mother tortoise
just by glancing at them
feeds and cares for her young in water.
"But Mother, we haven't
even a single look from you
and now we climb the skies."
Yes, she had only seen her sons with her ears.
These cries of theirs, and to them
she shuts her ears
just as she shut her eyes.

Wounded and crippled by war
he asks for a single mouthful of water
but sees before him his dead brothers
dragged around and gnawed on
by dogs, wolves, crows.
Likewise she saw
in the vast expanse before her eyes

a monstrous cow from hell
chewing human cud.

Before she was a river
her husbands
like cattle at a market,
the council
like frozen heaps of ash,
the blind king's court
apparently carved from stone.
She saw slaves
not men or women
and closed her eyes before her husbands,
plugged her ears before the council,
and sealed her lips before the court.

"Fire inside. Prayer.
Keep it as a weapon.
Inside.
We will return.
To choose."
So they left them
under a tree.
And the look of them.
When they set out
for another country.

She followed them.
Her husbands.
Who looked like
fires recently dampened.
And she coming behind
a pillar of black smoke.

The row of clouds, evening, red edges.
I imagine epic battles.
Histories, feuds, and fortunes.
She braids her hair.
A blood lust. To drink up
her enemies.
Again. And again.

Death also goes away.
And keeps on going.
One thing after another.
Bad to worse.
Every possibility a disaster.
Happiness itself an unhappy thought.
Things wanting to go wrong forever.

"I hope we are friends forever.
That our children marry one another."

Hearing the king say this
made the other king smile,
then stop. He looked down
at what he wore.
He felt where the gash
had been.
Made by the other king
who'd thrown dice at him.

"Win! Win! Win!
Live forever!
Nothing can touch you!"
That's how he went at it.
Death listened to their prayers.
But chuckled to himself.
And as he attacked
Death, slack jawed,
mumbled to himself
"Sure, okay, that's how it'll be
if he's still alive tomorrow."

"Be certain I will return the winner
having flattened the field.
God has told me this is so.
He said this early in the morning."
But by dusk he'd been kicked

and trampled by the entire field.
Then moaned
"A message from god
is very tricky
and can destroy a man
down to his root."

You could hear the name
of the dead man.
on both sides
Yet it was more of a party
than a grieving.
It made you wonder
where this illusion came from.

His good luck protected him.
But the self-same luck took it away.
This very mechanism
stuck his wheels in mud
as though to remind him
of when he said:
"Victory is mine.
Look! Here! At it!"

Beads scattered from a broken necklace.
Like that, his brothers died.
Freezing rain slipping through the fingers,
his reputation disappeared.
Left with a shattered thigh
and still he seeks fame and fortune
who keeps on saying
"Here I am. Come and get me."

"There's nothing I can do
to prevent the destruction of this family.
Yet they call me 'Terrible.' Why? They
claim I was never
a part of their history."

That old blind man
is still around
and keeping pretty powerful company.
It was he who said,
"Come, my son, put your arms around me
and make me happy."
All the while telling himself,
"You bastard, come here
and let me squeeze you to death!"

"I have no good news to tell you
only an unending story,
the death and destruction of your sons."
Hearing this, the blind man
already engulfed, saw his sight
grow darker, and darker yet.
Pitch black.

"This man, his father, and grandsons,
and all his followers
are crushed between my jaws. Look!"
Whoever saw this
fell to the ground.
A long time ago.
Earth itself
provides the jaws.

Let loose.
No longer connected to anything.
The overwhelming and terrible conflict
is history, a distant memory.
As though at the ledge of a mountain,
the foot slips, the voice echoes.
Where is the unfaltering step?

"I pray to god.
And am glad.
I offer my hand.
And my blood."
Bowed he left.
And god felt shame.
It overcame
and overwhelmed him
endlessly.

Hard work made the god
and those that bowed before him
whose hidden fears
lie deep in the forest,
whose hand
is wounded.

The bow plucked
and the mountain quakes.
They flee and fly to heaven
where they hide.
"You should be proud.
Your pupil plays well."
But no, he can only think of
a bloody hand.

"Attack us for worshiping idols
but tell me,
with all your prestige
and fame
could you teach us
what these little mud statues have?"

Alone, someone
leans forward
bent into a huge burden,
a dead weight
lashed across his forehead.
The mouth that screamed curses at him
is gone for good.
This grief has no release.
Wide-eyed, beady, vacant he sees
this overblown, restless world show forth.
Untouched by everything but
his suffering.
His heavy steps. The load on his head.
Unshared.

Say their names.
How many? Who?
So many. But each pops
like a bubble in Time's river

and is swept away.
Thousands of gods.
Worshiped. Adored. Adorned.
Then swept aside.
You only have to look
to see this happen again and again.
Up they come, the new ones,
right out of the earth.
Hardly born, already at the edge
of Time's black pit.

Be careful. If you happen
to put your foot down on a battlefield.
Be careful where you step.
That lump of mud might turn out
to be your father's head
who threw down his weapons
and wailed, "My son! My son!"

They say: "This is the way!"
"This is meant to be!"
"This is God's will!"
And the deathless god
hears this and laughs.
Sometimes thunder in the clouds.
Sometimes in roaring oceans.

Here we go again.
You have seen through millions of years.
The government set upon dead presidents
is the ledge to set the next president on.
And having seen this, do you look at them all,
a parade of the dead and alive
with their coming and going,
as nothing more than place markers?
Or market place?

God, you live on this earth deathless.
In fact, you are a traveler here
going from one place to another.
But think about this, all the people
whose lives are brief
yet they are stuck to the land,
even as it slips out from under them
and they die. What is that about?

Trying to find out what lasts,
he gets life's favor.
Searching for the philosopher's stone,
many an ordinary piece of rock fooled
him.
Walking forever,
he has seen enough of what this world has to offer.

Exhausted, he keeps on going
searching for nothing in particular.

Whose tears are these.
Are they cried in court before a judge?
Or in a dark and unforgiving wood?
With this thought in mind,
I look at a drop of dew,
and say, "This is not a pearl,
not a jewel."

This fire needs to be put out
as slight as it seems.
But to blow it out
makes it flare up like a funeral pyre.

They came to him in jail
and asked had he heard,
that the kid had killed the boss
and knocked over another operative,
stamped out a whole gang,
and purified the waters of a nearby river?
It takes away the breath
and takes away what binds.

"How far away do you live?
How long ago? Suddenly there.
Before me in this cell."
Was it in a dream
she held her son?
The chains on her arms
turned into garlands of flowers.

When he saw inside his hut
an immense gilded palace
he was suddenly shy.
"Where do I sleep?
Eat? What do I sit on?"
Here he was, a stranger in his own home.
With fond memories
of his old hut.

Who can outdo him?
Even his complexion
is darker than any one else's
due to his lack of fidelity.

What about these people?
They set up altars to god
and blindly worship him

completely unaware that he
stands beside them
raising his hand to smash
these altars
but pauses, stopped by the thought
of his life,
a thin line traced upon still waters.

When she saw her shadow on the wall
a little girl hugs her mother's legs.
When she saw her shadow on the wall
a young woman saw her husband's there as well
and sorrow and fear shook her.
When Death came she opened the door
and welcomed him like a long lost friend.
She was very calm.
If only we knew how she did that.

Crossing between this world and another
he was very confused
by what he thought
was and wasn't
real.
When drawn back
by the hook and line
of this familiar world

he was forever anxious.
That glimpse of something else
was a knife to split him in two.
How ever long he lived
he had that fresh cut
and it bled and bled.

When Death came to her
she sweet-talked him
out of taking her.
Then there was the young man
who struck up a conversation
during which, much to Death's embarrassment,
the young man discovered Death's secret.
After two such instances
Death refuses to give anyone an audience.
Instead he sneaks around now,
carrying a noose,
and jumps his victims from behind
without any regard for right or wrong.

No words tell it.
Nor ear hear even if told.
Trying to, however, made him a joke
and although the secret had been his
eventually he came to doubt he knew it.

And Death who worried that his news
had been carried up to the living
drew an easier breath
when he saw that young man's uncertainty.

"I took off my clothes, piece by piece
until with the last to go
my soul was free,
stripped by birds.
(Well, they were actually dice changed into birds.)"
Hearing this the godess
said: "Free?
Not so easy. There is still
the body to go."

His wife's caresses
once made his mind a tree
filled with fireflies
after a heavy rain.
But that was then. Now
he wants to leave her
and that same mind of his
is a nest of wasps.
"No, no, no!
Let this stinging fire
burn up all thought of her."

"My son, I'm sending you
straight into the enemy camp.
How do I feel about this?
Overjoyed? Or worried?"
These were not things he said
but could be read in his eyes,
the tears there.
So it was this the son took with him
as he left.

He knew he was his enemy's son
but took him as a pupil anyway.
He knew how his daughter loved
his enemy's son.
And he ignored all this for a long time.
But now rants and raves.
His own foolish neglect remains
the simple wine of this situation.

"You tricked and fooled me,
disguised. I lost everything I had.
But I don't care about that.
What worries me
is how what you've done to me
ruins all worthy intentions."

And he bowed his head
to stare at his feet.

Some are famous eventually.
Some get done what they want to.
But then there's the solitary figure
weeping tears of blood
forever cursing his lot.

Under rigid control
the teacher admitted
he was uncomfortable
talking about this.
But the parrot in his cage
by the door
cries out loud
"I won! I won!"

His whole political career
passed before his eyes.
With all humility, he said,
"Politics? Ethics?
Like a parrot
I said what I was told
until the cocoon

of what the public wanted to hear
bound me in silk
and made me its fool."

"Your pride will reap the
fruits of your distain for me!"
He cried and walked away.
And behind her smoked
the ashes of her destiny.
She had no idea.
Nor friends beside her.
No one even knew she'd been cursed.
Nor how this misfortune could be lifted.

They suffer torture
eyes wide open,
pain even a god would fear,
hiding himself at the bottom
of a river.
We hear about these things.
They are history
as well as what's going on
all around us.
But they make so little sense.
How great the small is.

How little confidence the powerful have.
Upside down. The whole world.

Only his head is left.
Yet he doesn't have any problem getting around.
Why all the fuss? He swallowed the sun and moon.
So what?
Pretty selfless, not much of him to care about.
What was once his body burns
upon his head.

His stepmother used to beat him
until finally he ran away
in a burst of flames
to find somewhere beautiful to hide.
Just so he still keeps his own company.
Even in heaven
he avoids contact with the gods.

"How come this boy, and no more than that
is out to get what no one can get
by knowing alone. What no one can get
by prayer or sacrifice even."
So remarkable was this
that the seven wise men

looked toward heaven
and walked in circles around him.

I'm not sorry to see
my head bowed to
a wise man born from a simple kettle.
But it surprises me to see
my snow-capped brother
laughing at me,
thinking he's laid me low
by his own strength.
Nonetheless I have to bear this.

This son whose head was never visible
but cloud covered
provided the gods happy shelter.
In fact, they abandoned heaven.
This same son now lives in the deep ocean
and has the affection
of water animals
who never tire of playing with him.
And he is not the least bit ashamed.

This son living in the ocean all the time now,
your wings weigh you down

and if you try to raise your head
so far below
the angry waves
beat upon your head.
Yes, hiding here you escaped
the god's lightening bolt
but might as well otherwise be dead.
A bloodless, weaponless killing.

A tree withers
in the shade of another and greater.
Two can't reach their full growth side by side.
The driver of the sun's car
has become forever lame.

Despite their deathless lives
the gods envy the devils,
wanting what they have,
unable to bear what little
any one of them has.
But then
gods are
what they are.

How often is your choice inappropriate?
Which, forgive us, makes us
doubt
your most intimate
associations.

Famous for her anger,
something like a cross
between
an eagle and a snake.
And just as famous
for her fickleness.
How can the god she loves
wander very far
from his home
at the bottom
of the sea.

Her delicate flesh
and definite come-on
made his skin break out
into eyes, a thousand.
Though they itched
and wept. As much
a curse as a
gift from god.

When he went to live in the woods
the lamp, the only watcher in that dark night,
folding its smoke into fingers wrote
upon the air in large clear letters
a history of loss.
The son and wife
left behind, on whose behalf
apparently he shed not a tear.

He
seated in the temple
watching the crowds
bow and scrape, folded
hands, with wide open
souls
remembers
with sudden pangs
the river bottom
where turtles and fishes
and who knows
what other
water animals
heaped upon him
insult after insult
so that he pulls
down the garlands,

scarves, icons, candles
piled up around and on him
to sigh, "O fickle Fortune,
none of this is mine,
I turn it all over to you."

At one time he denied her
and let her burn to ashes,
a handful.
But now she overpowers him
and he is trapped in
her lack of a body
as though they were both
pent up
in the same cage.

Swallowing poison
this one became a champion.
But that one
drinking nectar
nearly died.
So who can tell
what happens
since apparently
the same thing but different people

produces unpredictable
results.

You hold in you
both deadly poison and refreshing nectar.
When asked about these
you smile and keep still.
Does this indicate, perhaps
death on the one hand
and immortality on the other?

Ah, my mountain,
you avoid attention,
your head hung low
forever. But ever hoping
the prophet would appear
as promised.
But when you think about it
these prophecies are merely lies.
So now, who can trust
even the best of men's word.

"As solid as his brow is
would it be able to bear

a flood of me. Fast and
furious cascading from
above." Saying this
the goddess came down to earth
somewhat hesitantly.
And when she saw his face
blushed.
And softly stepped
upon his forehead
taking the form of snow.
A shower and silent mounds
of white petals.

BEEN THERE

you call the people who steal
your ideas thieves
yet take great delight in
moonlight
the sun's faint facsimile

the corrupt spoil all well-being
even in their downfall
think about it
the cobra injures the branch
it lies along and chews
losing its own fangs

the fork-tongued snake
may strike or not
but the many-tongued
nature of unrestrained evil
delivers its blow instantly

despite being ignored
nonetheless
honor is bestowed

when a crow
finds something
to eat in a cemetery
left as an offering
by mourners
at a recent burial

so say
the snake charmers
our god
our lord
everything's
very beginning
sway
show us
evil
inside your hood

I want to make Jesus
a shirt out of
sunlight
and rugs out of
the rainbow
for his bride
but dream about
my own coat

being made of straw
and thrown away
an old story

gold scraped beaten and burnished
weighed with potatoes
in the other pan
shocking
gold sought after prized and worshiped
in this world
but how philosophical
to set in equal measure
with potatoes
making it earthy
but maybe
this is some kind of con
what the hell
is there any wisdom
untouched by dubious
intentions

completely oblivious
the wine salesman on a binge
peeks between his fingers
through the keyhole of his psyche

and sees so it seems
someone looking in

this hay stuffed scarecrow
these animals all run away from
is made of the stuff they graze on
little do they know
so show us scarecrow
the power of your arm
the grace of its blow

tossed by stormy seas
these rats were sure
their ship was sinking
into the ocean
and deserted it
by the dozens
bless them
the waves grew calm
after a while and steady
and those rats
like a grief gnawing at the heart
vanished completely

the honey in your poems
silences the cuckoo
and stops the bees buzzing
though they won't pay you a dime
there might be someone
who hears you

if you think of saffron
being crushed
or the pounding
of sugar cane
think of what
total annihilation
brings

a blow struck
yet the wound won't heal
even after years
how lucky are animals
their wounds
are skin deep
like a stain on cloth
they aren't life-long
a whole long life

this dull dime
from pocket to pocket
moves through the world
like a metaphor
for what
life may be
going on and on

"through learning
we are released
and endure"
in that pompous
academic's
words
you hear
the clink of loose change
the folding of bills
"learning works for me
it puts the spin on big ideas"

I used to own very little
but now that I don't
I'm struck by just how much
and it's all alike

I used to watch the rich
going in and out of their big houses
their big cars
when I didn't have a cent
and when I had a little
it seemed to me the world
was better that way
somehow different
at each step

only a memory
stupid to keep looking for it
like a lost ring
or worse stomp around
with clenched fists
as though that could stop
the stuff in dreams
from slipping though
your fingers

in my dreams I am rich
I guess to give me an appetite
for that life
so that although I am poor
I think of myself as
having once been wealthy

the upshot of which
is that I've lost to greed
the peace of dreaming
as well as the peace
of waking

a poet said
pointing to a dark spot
on the moon
that's black money
carried there by
dead traders
who fled earth
but in fact
those thieves
and smugglers
left their loot here on earth
and paid interest on that sum
with their deserted bodies
that poor innocent moon
must put up with these stories
that cause him such deep grief

cut and broken
shaped and chipped
stone becomes statue

yet we hear about
how every road
is lined with
unhewn
gods

everybody remembers money
even at the point of death
even so tirelessly charity
works away
past
the last
breath

money slips through
even the most careful of fingers
or is lost
like a
dream
when you wake

because I am poor
my friends avoid me
but now the god tells me
poverty is your best friend

the earth turns to mud
with our over-exaggerated weeping
a pale glow abounds
from our much too wide smiles
cloud and fog fills the sky
with our empty promises
for a handful of this or that
what role is there
we won't assume
false note we won't sing
or game we won't play

hard times have their rewards
they are the outward mirror
of our lives
just as they are
an inward source
to call upon

whatever we call you
fate fortune destiny
you've been like a magician
at a kid's birthday party
and shown me
how this world is
and isn't

seemingly large
or small
important or
trivial

look at him
doesn't give it a second thought
and marches on
or him
he dawdles
and has to be egged on
or there's the guy
who runs ahead of everyone
get rid of him
all this is like poetry
it can't be compared to anything else
it has its own internal logic
it hints

the stuff we want
and wait for
we soon loose interest in
and put aside
or neglect
you can see this
in the billowing empty clouds

that trail across an autumn sky
or last night's candle this morning

"doctor please I don't want to die"
after a few weeks of treatment turns into
"death please take this doctor"
it's this kind of thing that makes it clear
we neither want nor know what we know or want
birds used to be caught
in nets
now men not birds
are snared
in meaningless
empty shiny
language

that fire
burning in the depths
of an immense ocean
makes us wonder
yet we wander around
completely unaware
that in the words
politicians use
opposite meanings
also hide

I hear the words loud and clear
but making no sense at all
so why not a mute
moving his lips

"our great president
your power dims the sun
your prowess leaves the moon
dead
as a peacock feather's eye"
this praise
binds their spinners
each word a link at a time
to the payroll

when I see people today
whose cars or watches
or whatever bear logos
that might've once been
on the banners of kings or
warriors who no doubt
were no less aggressive or
greedy I think of the things
the images imagine
how much are they
a part of all this

she stumbles
at each word
nor can she remember
what she just said
is she drunk
no it is the hatred
in her speaking

if what you say
no matter how loudly
or sweetly
can't be understood
then it really isn't said is it
but what you say
and don't want heard can't
be really meant can it

while words can be
charming and sophisticated
talk can be poetry
and an arrow
to pierce both
heart and mind

there's time and place
which influence the meaning of a word
nonetheless that meaning
seems to hold
in a way that makes us ask
about meaning itself
today tomorrow the day after
or is the word
a kind of rock star
up there to be
for the moment what we want
or is it simply empty
ready to fill with the meaning we provide
in other words a mirror
to show us what we want to see
our idea of word or meaning is so weak
that we must pity
listening itself
but also ask
if once they weren't
not so much the same thing
but at the same place
at the same time

interesting to find out
that in some languages
the same word

was used
to mean its opposite
rich man poor man
only the tone of voice
or a gesture
indicated which
was which

we have plenty of questions
yet the expert we ask
answers with still more
questions
brushing ours aside
and what can we say
when he says
"no more questions
everything clear"
again what can we
say when he says
"I've told you so"

being awake itself
gets the fire going
coaxing flame
from an ember

a burning memory
that at night sleep
blows out and eases

the dark watches
what the day
does at night
while the day
condemns the dark
for what goes on then
but the dark
simply laughs away
this scorn
bursting into flame

washing away all care
making dreams come true
good sleep
surrendering everything it has to us
but that poor god
with a thousand open eyes
is deprived of this

despite the earth's spin
its inhabitants
appear still to themselves
while whirling like a top

a man steps
into the river
when a boulder
calls out to him
why would you want
to swim
in this
illusion

the new look
and the old scattered
all over the ground
but be careful to make up
covering yourself entirely
so that someone clever
and looking to knock you down
doesn't notice your feet are gone
that that's mud
and clay
where they were

abundant crops can't happen
until the ground is ploughed
jewels don't appear
until the earth is gouged
flesh and blood hide their essence
until a wound offers it up

a fine mist
falls from the clouds
and is gone
before it reaches
the desert heat
a thousand thoughts
vanish into thin air
before the mind
can grasp them

fame and fortune
are like moonlight
their touch
makes even the darkest soul
appear pale and delicate
but when they take away their grace
what seemed sleek and silvery
resumes its true color
and rightful place

what will be
rises then falls
gains and loses
a glance can change everything
good luck or fire
so that a dog
can wind up with a lion's share
or a lion be tied to a post
barking at the air

watch the water wheel
in this garden
slowly turn
and its constancy
broken
by that sudden
gush

this bug with all the legs
can hardly budge an inch
yet the sun hasn't a foot to stand on
and carries himself
from one end of this world
to the other
what could be more
upside down than

having too much to work with
or nothing at all

humans are clever
at getting things done
but how without weapons
like a fire without sticks
can the beast be killed
by sheer skill alone
not claws not teeth

in a high castle
a carving
on a dark red stone wall
shows us scales
held in perfect balance
and anyone who sees this
sees "justice" depicted there
but from behind that wall
comes an almost inaudible
murmuring
"This red is the red of tongues cut out of
the mouths of my enemies
who thought they could
speak out against me"

I notice in town
wolves and wild men
chasing innocent deer
hiding in the leaves
waiting in the shadows
and I also see hunters
with their handsome fresh faces
chasing these wolves and wild men
faster and with better weapons
it remains to be seen
whether the woods
or the town
is more dangerous

a time of great spirituality
descends upon us
somewhat suddenly
apparently god is seeking donations
just as his devotees
at the start of any project
proclaim
"to take one must first give"
and I assume both
they and god
will profit accordingly

let the experts claim
"we've got the measure of everything
old or new dead or alive
the last word the why
of what never before made sense"
but do they know about that measuring
which can't help ending up
with just what it's looking for

long ago
the men on earth then
said
"we'll construct
a stairway to the stars"
and the animals on earth
asked "how"
"standing on each other's shoulders"
and the animals laughed
but eventually
a stairway to the stars
was built
a few steps at a time
pulling one leg up
then the other

this mirror
which flatters anyone who gazes into it
represents an ideal
in the curious habits of this world
when the real ideal
would be a mirror
that made even
gold
cringe
at its imperfection

you hear the brutality
of human beings
mentioned by academics
also their restless intelligence
could that be why
animals lower their gaze
and the gods are unblinking

does it pay to listen to
good advice
to get self respect
stay humble
to get rich
give lavishly
to get smart

forget what you know
to get free
stay within bounds
does that make sense
ask for an apple tree
and they point out a pear

three monkeys sit on three steps
"make what you see unseen
what you hear unheard
what you say unsaid"
another three monkeys sit
on another three steps
somewhere else
"undo what is unseen
unheard unsaid"
neither here nor there
yet before and around us
thousands of things

we make ourselves unhappy
wanting what we haven't got
that's no surprise
even the sun
chases after his own shadow

a raised eyebrow and they flee
or they are light-headed
when they see her foot step
or she pushes aside
whoever reaches to touch her dress
though there are a few
she embraces only to brush aside
who is this
a movie star a whore no
she is hope
who makes us chase
after her

does the keystone
consider itself
higher up
somehow
luckier
than the flagstone

in his envy of humans
god has created fate
we have the ability to fly
but creep
we can cross vast oceans
but trace the flight of birds

we walk anywhere we want
but why not go to hell
quick now

god forgive
those who can't see
beyond your temple door
their faith blinds them
and so do
the raging bulls
stomping their feet
at the edge of this yard
they set up a stone found in the field
and built a church around it
and worshipped there
for ages
though the stone eventually cracked
under the weight of their prayers
so they simply threw it away
which made god himself
get rid of
the pride he held for his role
as maker
and breaker of creation

stepping down
on what is certainly
firm ground
someone splashes
into a river
carefully making his way
through a swamp
someone trips
down some steps
what is going on
these are illusions
made by an illusion

covering
the top of a mountain
so high even the horses
that draw the sun
stare up at it in amazement
are acres of
rough grass
this is called patience
however that may be
the little snail
or tiny salamander
says to the huge
whale in the ocean
"forgive and forget"

inside us still
just like in a forest
there are high flying eagles
creeping and crawling snakes and beetles
roaring lions and flocks of timid sheep
part of us we are part of it
all the way back
to our first mother and first father
in the wild

happy day my easy friend
in your satisfaction
bowing down to a piece of rock
smeared with red dye
putting up with whatever happens
certain it's all meant to be
and a blessing
never for a moment
looking into it

I'd like to ask
those who tell me
to keep to the path of devotion
is devotion the same thing as acclaim
which god forbid is nothing more than fruit
which will rot soon enough

in these matters aren't
man and god the same
won't both eventually
tear me apart

stupid as it sounds
I'm asking
"if desire is the
seed the tree springs
from aren't there
trees that are bitter
prickly or leafless"

what I taste as sweet and like
someone else finds sickening all
experience it seems
involves difference
because of our own diversity
which makes me wonder
if the idea of a reliable
definition
isn't an illusion

I never know
if those who

believe
get any sleep
but I see them wipe away
the occasional tear
while those who
don't believe
can't sleep
and never shed
a tear

I'm not sure
who I'm playing
though I've
got the part
but not the plot
nor even really
what it's
about

when I die
all the air in my lungs
will leave and rise
to heaven
while the rest of me
will return
to its various elemental

natures
but what else will be left
here or there
that was me
thinking about this
recently something inside me
cried out all day
and all night
"who am I"

once upon a time
there was a deer
who ran after
a fog of gold
chasing
what isn't there
just as time itself
once pursued
both the hunter
and his quarry
both of whom in turn
sought nothing more
substantial than a fine rain
but the real question is
is there a hunter
on the trail
of time itself

life makes
what you first see of it
a bit puzzling
keeping the real
mystery
deep inside

here we are
without any sense of what's going to happen
much less a memory of what has
envious of
that life with
a beginning middle and end

sometimes disease
sometimes fire or poison or whatever
the direction unseen
captures us
and brings us to its big emptiness
where time is completely lost
and has neither breathing room
nor end

wealth
you have always been

faithless and
capricious
never to be counted upon
yet that lesson you teach
is hard to learn
that what we have
we haven't earned
but got from your
good whim

forever it seems
we hear about
the whims of fame and fortune
their easy come their easy go
the hard lesson
they teach
everything we have
is a gift
we haven't earned a thing
just wait and they
will desert us
not if but when

the actress plays
a young girl in love
a mother who murders her baby

an old woman who cannot die
what a range
of feelings
the breathtaking
gestures
yet in all this diversity
the marvelous alone
dominates
it is the witness
to this wonder
we must admire
who takes such pleasure
in this variety

there's a story
about a decapitated head
gobbling up the sun and moon
to which
there is some truth
how we humans look to heaven
trying to pull ourselves
out of the mud of our lives
yet are haunted by
strange longings
that pop up
out of nowhere

thought
soars above the sky
one moment
then plunges
beneath the ocean the next
it outdoes the wind
whose measured pace
space contains

the stars and clusters of stars
planets the milky way
all hang from the branches of
a cosmic tree
and though the gods try
they can't pick them
nor know
how far these branches spread
so how could we on earth
figure out
their root

often the desert
will show the traveller
shade cool water
an oasis
and this mirage

isn't meant to trick him
but ease the mind
on its dry trek

"listen I am the purpose you're looking for"
the resonant voice inspires confidence
from the start
and the way he moves his hands
mesmerizes
we are so caught up in this
that we follow to arrive
in a dark uncertain place
just as he vanishes
behind a screen

I saw it in a glance
in a dream
not when I was completely awake
this longing knows no let up
and won't listen to common sense
with its reasonable answers

time has no end
nor can one imagine
the size of earth

even so they're
no larger than a life

it's worthwhile
no doubt
to think about stuff
but who
in this world
can take apart
the wind

this great big truck
as it goes down the road
the friction from the wheels
grinding time's pavement
makes sparks that are stars
yet there are those
whose vehicle is rock-like
and as they lumber along in it
imagine themselves
as highway gods

in a frenzy
we gather up
moments

and fragments
and prepare our lives
for success
yet every one
of these plans
ends with death
but we go on
making them

what do you gain
giving in
completely
to pleasure
yet what do you get
avoiding it
altogether

I flew from this to that
like a bee
and paid no attention
to what I got or
what I wanted to get or
if it was worth getting at all

I wasn't nor will be
merely froth
if this is the answer
why ask
or if dark
stay blind
and avoid
the question

looking wants to take shape
but is prevented
by some apparent
outside force
looking is looking for
a final unit
but turns away
from emptiness
and therefore
will never see anything
worth seeing
so it makes sense to say
"sight merely decorates
a face"

the most we can know
about this world

is "not"
and the "nothing" that is
is a delusion
the power all this
comes from
hides in the making
which is and isn't
sleight of hand

what ever happened
changes beyond all recognition
so does what is
and what has yet to come
they all gleam
in a flash of lightning
a grand parade
moves across my closed eyes
clouds pushed and broken
by the storm

they come to the ocean's shore
and fate stops them in their tracks
they climb the highest mountains
and fate freezes them there
or fate displays horizons
that will never be reached

they are all held
the way spokes are checked
by the wheel's rim

as the mists rise
becoming clouds
they mount the wind
horses now
when a storm kicks up
now stallions
climb higher
vomiting blood
on the edge of death
is that our life
here on earth
written in the sky

people go about their business
in any number of ways
but look at their god
who faces four directions
at once

life is like
a Ferris wheel

eventually we return
to where we were
well maybe not

life is like
a spiral staircase
where we never
get back
to where we were

I was certain this
was the holy of holiest places
here my eyes
would witness glory
when something inside me
said
"don't enter
through this door"

our delight in this life
one moment vanishes
into thin air the next
a speck of what happened
the spider web of wanting
always comes up with

something new
forever a magic carpet
in the air

there then not there
almost like the law
of cause and effect
are the people I know
or have known
with one exception
a friend of mine
who will remain beside me
until my last dying breath
the "I" I call myself

the past is dead
the present slips by
what about the future
will it be any different
if we look forward to it

the new
soon remains so
in talk alone
and certainly dead
in time

shown this
yet refusing to believe
in illusion
you must be
blind

here I sit for hours
throwing a net into the sea
to catch fish
but all I get are waves
and ripples that swell
and disappear
capturing my attention
in the strings
and knots
of my imagination

I've gone all over the globe
talked to the hills
the trees the air
and not one of them
could show me
how to take one step
then the next
and one after that

hills valleys rivers caves
call out to my heart
then echo in my thoughts

"there is no one to ask for directions
not a place to stay in sight
an empty horizon
a dense wood
where now"
so he makes himself
a friend out of clay
someone to talk to
and sets forth again
but is abandoned
soon enough
the waters of a mirage
washed his friend away
and he calls out after him
filling the air with sadness

you can see here where
a sword struck and where
a shield blocked the blow
but you can't see who
held that sword or shield

whoever it was
who wanted
to grow as huge
as the universe
did and to this day
is lost in looking
for himself

time blinks
and his open eye
is day
night
his eye shut
however much we think we can
we can't
measure him except
with day and night
which are his
anyway

where is that mysterious
hand
that does and undoes
our dreams and wishes
that pulls down

the walls
around us

somewhere I saw this
a granite ball
which could be moved freely
inside a stone lion's
open jaw
earth is like that
free yet contained

the vast reaches above us
is only half of what there is
the other half is hidden
under us and we are left
to wonder what will last
and what won't
in these seen
and unseen worlds

"don't overestimate your progress brother
give me a second and I'll be ahead of you"
my left foot following tells the leading right

several times
I thought the unknown
had been
just about
revealed to me
the real truth of which
is how loosely
it held me
having none of
the gravity of
say
a tree

walking straight ahead
my feet fight each other
yet I'm still able
easily
to get where I'm going

my foot lifts
and the ripples it made
disappear
but the water continues to circle
the other one
quickly and unknown

they say
there are people
who look into their minds
and see things
when I do that
I only see
dark colors

some try to define you
in the web of categories
using various shapes
and any number of names
though I don't know
who you are or how you are
or what you are
much less if you are
so being that uncertain
what good are shapes or names
to me or even you

a house however grand
or humble
palace or bungalow
both eventually
fall into ruin
time himself

sits on the beach
building castles
his waves will wash away

people dismiss what is
for what isn't
and what's done
is done for no reason
strong arms hug
pale shadows
all this show
of good intentions
inspires
little confidence
and the unborn ask themselves
why go through with it

we on earth
imagine gods
drinking deathlessness
and we say we worship them
when
what we really worship is
a guarantee
that we won't die
but be young forever

this fear vanishes
only in dreams
and in our envy

I'm told
about something
that can't be said or thought
and has nothing to do
with what makes us happy
or not
something outside of
our knowing
but what gets me
is that
it's still
something
I want

in my brain
I see
a flood of things
a huge fish makes a tidal wave
something creepy not quite a lion
not quite a man
opens its mouth
and utters silence

a beautiful young woman
dresses herself
but isn't quick enough
to completely cover
her nakedness
a tiny smiling baby boy
sits on a leaf
puts his toe into his mouth
floats out upon the vast ocean
my poor brain
is the mirror of this
endless unraveling
a sky in autumn
the clouds scud across
in patches

AIRS WATERS PLACES

Aegyptian Love Song

For MJW

I breathe the sweet breath which comes forth from thy mouth. I behold thy beauty every day. It is my desire that I may be rejuvenated with life through love of thee. Give me thy hands, holding thy spirit. That I may receive it and may live by it. Call thou upon my name unto eternity and it shall never fail.

Look around.

When you come to a city
you've never been to before.

What do you see?

Dry flat hunks of clay
with

they might be words

pressed onto them.

To make an inventory
a story

took seven hundred years.

✦

Knowing things like this
finds out other things.

Summer or winter. Stars
rise and set. Such a one

knowing these things
in particular practices

an art.

Despite second thoughts.

The stars add an uncommon lot.

✦

Say clearly.
A city. Winter
winds.

Plenty of water
but briny.

✦

Cold winds in summer.
Gone blind. A long life nonetheless.

The city faces which way?

✦

Water flows to the sun rising.
Clear, sweet smelling, soft.
Good to drink.

See it that way.

✦

Scarcely touched. Cloudy ponds.
Morning mist.

No direct sunlight.

Summer

yet cold breezes and heavy dew.

More like autumn.
Dawn and dusk
differ.

Rough, hoarse talking.

✦

Summer marsh. Still waters. Fevers.
Or waters with frog eggs in them.

Those that flow from hills.
Sweet and clear.

✦

Rain water. Snow melting.
Sun draws the light sweet water

that is rain. But all water
once ice never recovers.

✦

When we drink from rivers
or streams or lakes

we drink all sorts of waters,
sweet, harsh, salt.

The north wind gives them their strength.

✦

Autumn rain, mild winter.
Spring and summer seasonal.

✦

Some fatal. Some pass away. Some change.
Study. Look and see.

Be careful when autumn changes to winter,
winter to spring, spring to summer.

✦

A long story. Asia and Europe.
Courage, endurance, work.

Mild, beautiful, large.

the middle of sunrise.

To take great pleasure.

✦

Difference of soil and seasons.
Difference of people living there.

Mountains, forests, plains, meadows.
Some places trees cover. Others

bare and dry.

✦

This is the result of that
though no longer the case.

Want becomes need.

✦

Fens, woods, warm, humid. Much
hard rain. All year round. Life

amid water. Rough speech
made so by breathing cloudy air.

✦

Seasons lacking much difference
work against change and understanding.

Perhaps this is obvious. Maybe not.
Then there is the matter of undeciding.

✦

The women ride horses, shoot arrows,
throw spears, and remain virgins

until they kill three enemies then
marry. All their strength depends upon

the fullness of their right arm.

✦

Peculiar shape, not like anything else.
Prairie, rich meadows. Men live in wagons.

Houses on wheels. They eat boiled meat.
Cheese made of horses' milk.

✦

Ice and snow provide drinking water.
What wild animals there are
are small and few.

✦

Tawny from the cold, not the sun.
Parched.

✦

Soft, cold belly. Weak desire.
A slender body.

✦

Nothing is any more divine
than anything else.

Tired and cold, desire disappears.

✦

Height and shape owe
the seasons their changes.

Wild, alone, brave.
The captured heart

won't risk its love.

✦

Rivers carry off still waters
and rain. How we are

is where we are.

✦

Hippocrates. Akhenaton.
Paraphrase. Parataxis. Praxis.
Pretension.

✦

Its sweetness. Your breath takes away mine.
I look at your beauty every day.
I want loving you to give me a life.
Let me hold your hands, and your heart in mine.
To take it then live by it.
Say my name. This will last a long time.